Woodworking for kids

The Ultimate Guide to Introduce Kids to Woodworking.Step-by-Step instructions and projects to build for kids.

Contents

Introduction

Welcome to the last guide on how to introduce their children to woodworking. From the safety standards to be adopted while we are working, the choice of the right wood to use for work and the right tools to never make mistakes.

Few things are more exciting and meaningful than doing something by yourself. This is especially true for woodworking. What's more exciting is to find that your child has the same interest and desire to build things.

However, when working with young children, there is a good line between making fun or turning it into work. This is about how to introduce your child to woodworking, while still allowing you and your child to enjoy it.

Few things can frustrate young children more than not knowing what you are doing. Although you may want your children to comment on their building, plan your strategy before you start so that you don't have to continue to stop and reorganize and look for supplies and tools.

Just as excited as your child started building, start them slowly. Introduce them to the tools you will use and the tools you will use. You may want to show them what the project will look like after it is finished.

There are many woods available. Teach your children about different types of trees and educate them about trees and their value. Consider using cork, such as mahogany, white pine, fir or cedar.

Expecting young children to help you build a dressing table is unrealistic and can lead to frustration. It can make your child quickly get rid of the concept of carpentry. Start your child by building some small things so that your child can do a lot of work.

Don't let your children learn woodworking by using toy tools. If they are using real tools, they will be more likely to exercise safety. The tools you will use include hammers, saws, nails, sandpaper, paintbrushes, paint or varnish. Use the simplest saw, such as a hacksaw or a saw that pulls without pushing. With this type of saw, your child will find it easier to use and much safer. Ensure that all tools are sharp and in good working order. Sharp tools can get work done faster and earn more respect.

In fact, this should be listed at the top because safety is paramount. Not only must you teach your child about safety, but you must always respect the tools. Make sure to use a vise or clamp to hold the wood in place.

Although your child may want to do a lot of things, they can be there to help when needed. Let your children do what they can, but if needed, let them know that you are free.

Depending on the age of your child, you may find that they will quickly become bored or want to quit their job. Don't let this situation stop you from working on the project. You may find it helpful to set a time limit, don’t be afraid to take a break. You don't have to complete the entire project in one day.

SAEFTY

Carpentry safety is a serious problem. Whether you are a novice woodworker or an experienced professional, safety is the primary consideration when working on a project. For the people around, safety is also a crucial issue. By working together and paying attention to each other, everyone in the woodworking workshop can enjoy work safely.

There are always dangers in the woodworking environment, including sharp blades and drill bits, and corrosive power tools. Being in the store also exposes you to environmental hazards such as glue, paint and wood pellets. You are always at risk of electric shock or cuts by hand tools. Then there is a danger of loose clothing or hanging jewellery in a moving machine.

Although there are hidden safety hazards in the woodworking workshop, there are also gains. Woodworking is a good hobby or profession when you understand your surroundings and understand your hazards. Safe work also includes familiarizing yourself with your materials and equipment. Following basic safety rules will bring hours of enjoyment, which makes safe work very meaningful.

However, your workshop is never a place for negligence or ignorance of safety rules. The key to ensuring safety in the woodworking workshop is awareness and compliance. Safety is more than just due diligence. Every time you enter a store and start using tools, you must be safe. One of your commitments is to keep learning safety procedures. For this reason, we bring you these woodworking safety tips.

Glasses

Without vision, it is almost impossible to do woodworking projects. It is also difficult to work without fingers and toes. In the woodworking workshop, every part of your body has certain risks. Your first line of defense is to wear personal protective equipment or PPE, such as safety glasses and protective gear.

Your standard woodworking PPE must include safety glasses. Under the right conditions, this can be safety glasses with side shields or even a full-face mask. However, please make sure that your glasses comply with OSHA standards. Poor vision protection is a bad investment.

Your personal protective equipment kit should include hearing and respiratory protection. Ear protection ranges from earplugs to earmuffs. You should use a respirator suitable for your task. It may be a disposable dust mask when cutting wood, or it may be a HEPA filter unit when dealing with toxic fumes.

Wear appropriate clothes

Appropriate clothing is also part of your personal protective equipment. Your carpentry dress code should enforce that the clothes you wear in the store are not inherently dangerous. Loose and loose clothing is the worst offense when tangled and tangled in a mobile device.

You always want to balance comfort and unrestricted conditions, while not being too hot and too irritating. Long-sleeved shirts and full-length pants are safer than shorts and T-shirts. Safety clothing is also suitable for wearing gloves under appropriate conditions and wearing appropriate footwear at all times.

Avoid wearing jewellery

The carpentry shop is not a place to hang chains or hang pendants. They are easily caught by rotating blades or rotating belts. Clamping the neck chain or lanyard in the mandrel can be life-threatening.

If you do have a special piece of jewellery, make sure not to use any tools. Keep the chain and lanyard invisible. You also need to assess whether the watch you wear or wear a ring on is harmful in the store. If you have any questions, please take it off and put it in a bag.

Disconnect power when changing blade or drill bit

Repairing any power tools or equipment that is still powered on is very dangerous. You should always think of plug-in tools as running tools. Every tool that is energized is waiting to consume its energy, and you are particularly vulnerable when changing blades or drill bits.

Make sure that you don't just turn off the tool with a switch when switching between drill bits or blades. Unplug the main power cord of the tool or turn off the circuit breaker at the power source. You can also lock the power supply to be extra careful. But no matter how you do it, before servicing, make sure that the power to the tool is completely turned off.

Do not use drugs or alcohol

This technique is self-evident. However, it is surprising that people with disabilities lose their judgment and decide to participate in woodworking projects. This is a dangerous decision that may result in serious injury.

Drinking before or during carpentry is foolish. The same goes for recreational drugs such as marijuana, because they can change your mental state. Then, avoid using legal prescription drugs, such as painkillers and antidepressants. No matter what kind of harmful substances, do not mix them with woodworking.

Use sharp blades and drills

It sounds counterintuitive, but a sharp blade is a safe blade. The blade becomes blunt, damage and wear are dangerous. The sharp blade can cut your wood quickly and leave a clean edge, almost no debris will pierce you. They also have less rebound, which is a dangerous part of woodworking.

The same is true for sharp drills. They will not get stuck and bound like boring debris. Buy high-quality saw blades and drill bits to get a high return on investment. The same goes for sending your blades and drills for professional reshaping. Never let your cutting tools become dull.

Check the wood for nails

Recycled wood is a very popular commodity. There are a few things about the look and feel of old wood that people like. However, for carpenters, something very dangerous lurks inside the old wood: the nails of primitive carpenters.

Before starting to use, make sure to always check the wood for nails or other fasteners. The visual inspection is good, you may catch embedded nails from the ventilation holes. However, if you are dealing with large amounts of recycled wood, the best option is to use a metal detector. Regardless of the system used, make sure to nail the nail before it falls on the saw blade or causes personal injury.

Against cutter

Almost every experienced woodworker knows to deal with cutter. This means bringing your work to the cutting tool as much as possible. It is safer to feed the workpiece against a fixed blade than to force it on the work surface. Working against the cutter reduces the chance of dangerous recoil.

However, many novice woodworkers and occasional hobbyists do not understand this important safety tip. That's because they have never learned to deal with knives. This does not seem natural and obvious. So next time you are in the shop, make sure to use cutting tools.

Use a single extension cord

How many times have you seen someone using a power tool and multiple extension cords twisted together? You may have noticed that they are experiencing a drop in current, not to mention the safety hazards of twisted wires. When one or more connections suddenly loosen, they also interrupt work.

The standard practice for power tools is to always use an extension cord when the power tool is used for a distance longer than the distance allowed by the wire to which it is connected. In addition, make sure to use a thick enough wire to provide enough current over a long distance. Your tool will help you because it doesn't take much effort. You can also perform safer and more accurate work without worrying about multiple saws or power tools having power.

Do not reach over a running blade

A blade within reach is one of the most dangerous things you can do in a woodworking shop. Your chances of slipping and engaging the blade are too high. Many woodworkers suffer serious or permanent injuries due to accidental contact when they hit the blades in operation.

Conversely, if you need to back up, take some time and effort to get close to the running blade. Even better, if there is such an important thing, turn off the tool and stop the blade. And, never forget how important the blade guard is. Make sure they are always in place.

Reduce interference

Sudden or constant distraction in your studio is not only annoying, but also dangerous. Distractions divert your attention and energy from what you do to other places. This may expose your hands and fingers and easily get injured.

There are many forms of distraction. Usually, this is someone accidentally entering your store suddenly. It can also be an external source, such as a broadcast program or vehicle noise. Mobile phones are one of the most distracting things in seminars today. To avoid dangerous interference, please keep your phone in another room.

Seek help when needed

This workshop reminds you to avoid serious injury. When you are dealing with heavy or bulky objects, don't try to make them idle. There is no shame in asking for help. It is not safe to try to complete tasks that exceed the limits of your body. You may suffer serious injuries, such as accidental contact with a running blade or muscle strain that can cause back pain. You can avoid this by asking for help when you need it.

Never work when tired

Fatigue is another form of damage. Tiredness will limit your focus and observation. Fatigue and drowsiness can affect your judgment and slow down your thought process, almost like drinking and taking drugs.

If you feel tired or sluggish, please consider working in a store again. Ask yourself if it is really necessary to perform the task immediately. Maybe it's best to take a nap or even postpone your project until you get a good night's sleep.

Clamp the workpiece firmly

Loose and unsafe woodworking materials can be dangerous. You may lose control of the workpiece and fly it away from the saw table, or table. That will become a missile in the store and make anyone in the line of fire vulnerable.

Always clamp the workpiece firmly. For small pieces, your hand pressure may be enough. However, for large components, make sure to use mechanical constraints. There are many clamp tables available, which allow you to be creative.

Take some time to read the tool manual before using the new tool

Do you know what they think about reading the instructions? Think about how you read the manual after you last purchased or adopted a new tool. Have you read and understood the content carefully?

The manufacturer encountered a lot of trouble in making the user manual. They do this because they want you to get the full benefit from the purchase. They also make manuals because they want you to work safely. Take time to read the manual before using a new tool. There's a lot of safety information in there.

Clean up sawdust

A clean shop is a safe shop, and a dirty shop is a dangerous place. A neat woodworking shop is a sign of a good carpenter.

Sawdust is an inevitable by-product in the woodworking workshop. However, it does not have to lie and cause safety hazards. You can slide on it, breathe, and let things block your view. If you always clean the wood chips, this will not happen.

Put the blade cover on the saw as much as possible

Most power tools with blades come with a cover provided by the manufacturer. They are there for a reason, and that is to ensure your safety. Keeping the blade cover allows them to do the job.

If you must remove the blade cover, make sure to do so safely. Turn off the power to the tool and keep the blade cover closed only when necessary. Then, replace the lid, and then resume work.

Do not try to release a stalled blade before the power is turned off

If you do a lot of woodworking work, you will experience stagnant blades. In fact, beginners are more likely to stall than veterans. That's because woodworking veterinarians know how to avoid blade stalls.

Long-term woodworkers also know that before the power is off, never try to release a stalled blade. This is the basic principle. A powered tool may start accidentally and seriously injure you. When releasing a stalled blade, make sure that the tool has no power supply.

When using a table saw, planer, band saw, table planer or pencil sharpener, please use a push rod or pad

When you use a table saw, band saw, table planer or pencil sharpener, the push rod and pad are both labor-saving and labor-saving. Fingers too close to rotating blades, belts and wheels are dangerous. This is also unnecessary.

Ensure your safety in the woodworking workshop and always use push pads or sticks when in close contact with cutting tools. These aids don’t need to be fancy or expensive, but they are necessary.

Use well-maintained tools

Maintenance tools are another sign of good woodworkers. You have invested a lot of money in the toolset and want to protect it. Routine tool maintenance is part of this process.

You will benefit a lot from using well-maintained tools. In addition to longer service life and better performance than worn equipment, well-maintained tools are also safer. Safety is part of your woodworking plan. Well-maintained tools can help you achieve your goals.

Use common sense

The best advice we can give you is to use common sense in the woodworking process. Slow down, pay attention and think about what you are doing. Make sure your work is wise.

Types of wood

Knowing the many different types of wood and their uses is very helpful in choosing the best wood for your next project. Whether you are building a house out of wood or just choosing wooden furniture for your own house, these wide varieties of wood will ensure you choose the wood you are satisfied with!

There are many different shapes and sizes of wood. Since wood comes from trees and there are many different kinds of trees, it is not surprising that we can use such a wide variety of wood to build buildings.

Before we study all the different wood species and their common uses, it is important to understand the three basic types of wood you may encounter. The three types are: softwood, hardwood and engineered wood. Each of these different types of wood can be used in many different ways.

Softwoods

Softwood is lumber and lumber milled from coniferous trees. Conifers are scientifically called gymnosperms and are any tree that has needles and produces cones. Examples of popular cork trees used in carpentry, construction, and furniture are pine, cedar, fir, spruce, and mahogany.

Is softwood softer than hardwood?

Contrary to popular belief, the reason why cork is not named cork is because they are "soft". Although it is true that some hardwood species are very hard and therefore more challenging to use, the difference between hardwood and softwood has nothing to do with the actual softness or whether a wood is more difficult to process. Many hardwoods are softer than softwoods.

How to use softwood such as pine, cedar, spruce, fir and mahogany?

Most cork is very strong and is commonly used in many different construction applications. Spruce, pine and fir (SPF) are usually sold in SPF size lumber at home improvement centers. These timbers are often used to construct new buildings and structures in practical architectural styles.

Many of these woods, especially softwoods from the cypress family, are known for their resistance to decay and insects. This makes trees such as cedar and mahogany ideal for exterior projects such as decorative panels and outdoor furniture.

Hardwood

Hardwood comes from any tree that does not produce needles or cones. These trees are most often called deciduous trees, and more scientifically called angiosperms. Hardwoods are trees that produce leaves and seeds.

Common hardwood species include oak, maple, cherry, mahogany and walnut. Hardwood species are not always stronger than softwood species, but many species are known for their beautiful and unique wood grain patterns.

There are also hardwoods that are not considered deciduous trees, such as bamboo and palm. These plants are scientifically called monocots, but they have many of the same characteristics as hardwoods, so they are usually classified as monocots. Bamboo and palm can sometimes fall into the next category of engineered wood.

Artificial wood: artificial wood products

The third type of wood you may encounter is engineered wood. Engineered wood is not produced naturally in the environment, but manufactured.

These boards are usually made of wood and have certain qualities or characteristics after treatment. These products are also called composite wood, and are usually made from wood waste from sawmills.

Artificial wood is usually processed through chemical or heat treatment processes to produce wood products that can meet certain dimensions, which are difficult to obtain from nature.

Popular examples of engineered wood include plywood, oriented strand board, medium density fiberboard and composite board. Wood veneers can sometimes be classified as engineered wood, because they usually need to be processed by special cutting techniques or by joining wood chips together to achieve a specific size or wood grain pattern.

Types of wood used in carpentry, furniture and construction

There are three main types of wood, but there are thousands of types of wood. In this section, we will introduce the most common wood you may encounter during construction and carpentry. For each type of wood, we will outline their common characteristics and what uses each type of wood is most suitable for.

All woods are listed in alphabetical order, so if you want to learn a specific type of wood, you can easily find it in this list.

Alder wood

Alder wood is a kind of hardwood that has gradually become popular due to its natural beauty, workability and versatility. It is more common in the Northwest Territories of California and Southwestern Canada. It belongs to the same family as Birch and therefore often shares similar applications.

Freshly cut alder wood looks almost white, but once exposed to air and sunlight, the quickly wood quickly turns into a warm honey brown. This medium-density wood usually has straight grain and is easy to carve, turn and process.

Wood also works well in various post-treatments. The surface of alder wood is very smooth when sanded, and it is easy to be stained or painted.

The diameter or height of Alder trees does not become larger, so if you need very large solid blocks, you need to consider this, as they may be more difficult and therefore more expensive to obtain.

Alder wood is often used in furniture manufacturing and cabinets. It is also a popular choice for photo frames and other decorative objects.

One of the more professional uses of Alderwood may be the hardware of electric guitars. Alder wood has a very clean tone and is difficult to replicate with other woods. In electric guitars, Alder is usually more suitable for tone than exotic hardwoods such as mahogany.

Ash

Currently, it is difficult to find ash wood, especially due to the recent Emerald Ash borer problem, which is an invasive pest that causes many trees to die prematurely. If you live in an area where volcanic ash trees are abundant and growing, it is easier to find this wood than if you live in a place without ash trees.

White wax has the same strength and properties as white oak, but if it can be found on a local logging farm near you, it is usually cheaper. Wood stains easily and can be used for many different types of projects.

Aspen

Aspen is a light-colored wood that can be painted and dyed well. This wood sometimes appears or feels vaguely grained.

Aspen is a hardwood that grows in North America, but it is sometimes difficult to find. Due to its limited overall availability, it is usually only used for very special projects that are very suitable for aspen.

One of the most professional uses of aspen wood is to build a sauna. Wood does not conduct heat and can tolerate moisture well through limited expansion or movement. Because it is not easy to conduct heat, it is sometimes used in the production of matchsticks. These characteristics are also the reason why Aspen is ideal for building drawer slides in furniture, because it can help reduce adhesion. This wood is also tasteless and tasteless, very suitable for making chopsticks and kitchen utensils.

Balsa wood

Balsa is a very light hardwood, usually used for hobby and handicraft type projects. Because balsa wood is not very strong, many senior carpenters often hold a negative view of balsa wood, but this balsa wood is often appreciated and has many practical uses.

Most of us first encountered balsa wood in our childhood architectural projects and model kits. Balsa wood may be a child's play for most serious woodworkers, but it may also be a catalyst for many people to engage in woodwork and construction.

This wood also has a rich history, especially because it was often used as a substitute for airplanes and ships during World War I and World War II.

Balsa wood is usually imported into North America from South and Central America. Balsa wood grows very fast, but has a relatively short life span. Most trees can only produce usable wood before the age of 10.

Wood is very buoyant, and many people are surprised to find that balsa wood is commonly used to build rafts, lifebuoys and other objects designed to float. Surfboards are a good example of exquisite works that can be made from balsa wood.

Balsa is a low-density wood, usually not strong. Therefore, for any type of project that needs to bear weight or pressure, many people prefer to choose bass wood and birch wood instead of balsa wood.

On the other hand, if you really need wood to build something that can break or break quickly, such as in theaters and movie stages, balsa wood is a good choice.

The wood grain can be easily painted or dyed for use as a veneer, thereby obtaining various appearances at a cheap price.

When assembling projects that use balsa wood, glue is usually used, because the board does not work well on nails or screws. It can usually be cut into thin balsa wood chips with a good tool or craft knife.

bamboo

Although technically bamboo is grass, not wood, it can be used to build many things due to the hardness and density of the plant stem. Bamboo grows in large numbers in tropical climates, and there are many different species available, which vary greatly from region to region.

The bamboo plant has a tall hollow stem. These stems can be used as they are, or they can be cut into very thin strips to make veneers.

The veneer products of the stem are made into engineered wood, such as plywood.

One might think that Bamboo is lightweight, soft and easy to bend or cut, but that is not the case. It is best to compare bamboo to hardwood red oak or maple, because bamboo has similar hardness and strength. High-density grass is sometimes difficult on tools.

Bamboo stems are especially suitable for garden furniture, garden decoration, fences and anti-theft screens. You can also see bamboo on cabinets, high-end furniture and even hardwood floors.

Part of what makes Bamboo resistant to outdoor rot is its natural waxy coating. If you want to dye, paint or glue the bamboo, you need to sand the wood first to ensure that the paint or glue sticks to the wood. If used outdoors, most bamboo should be sealed and protected for longevity.

Moisture can cause bamboo to expand or contract, so it is best to let the bamboo adapt to the environment before cutting, especially if you are in a drier and colder climate than the locally grown plants.

Basswood

Basswood is a very light beige wood with a very straight and tight grain. Wood that has been properly adapted and dried is not easy to warp or move.

Basswood is the hardwood favourite of carvers and carpenters. This is also a very popular choice for those who like miniature carpentry and architectural models. Turn carpenters often like basswood because it is easy to use and availability.

Wood also has no smell, taste or known allergens, thus making it a popular choice for food storage crates or even for use in kitchen appliances. Basswood is easy to find and usually budget friendly.

Basswood is difficult to dye evenly. In most cases, it is best to use only a protective clear oil coating to appreciate the natural appearance or paint the wood. Many decorating painters like to work on basswood projects because they get a very smooth effect once the primer is applied.

Beechwood

Beech is a type of hardwood that is commonly used for wood veneers, furniture and wood turning objects. This cream-toned wood has a consistent grain pattern, usually straight and tight, with occasional gray spots. The wood is light in color, but usually has a yellowish-red milky white hue.

It is a solid wood, known for its ability to bend easily with steam. Therefore, beech is an excellent choice for making any type of interior furniture, such as chairs and other curved pieces. However, this benefit also means that beech wood sometimes suffers from movement, shrinkage and swelling when exposed to high humidity or unpredictable moisture in the environment.

Beech wood is commonly found in pianos and is used in the bridge and pin blocks of piano mechanisms.

Beech belongs to the less expensive hardwood series and can be found in various sizes and veneers. As long as your tools are sharp, wood is relatively easy to process. If necessary, it can be glued and dyed easily.

birch

Birch is a hardwood that is easy to find, and is usually one of the cheaper hardwood species in local logging farms and home centers.

Birch is very strong and can be used for almost anything you can imagine. Many people use birch as a cheap alternative to Oak.

One thing to know about birch is that it is difficult to dye. Dyeing sometimes causes uneven spots. Therefore, if you plan to paint your project, birch is an ideal and economical hardwood.

California Sequoia

The California Redwood tree is a type of cork, known for its huge size and red color. It has a very interesting wood grain pattern and likes its Cedar cousin very much. Due to its weather resistance, it is very suitable for outdoor applications.

Mahogany is commonly used for railway connections and trestle bridges, and is also widely used for building retaining walls, decks and garden boundaries. Mahogany is also a suitable choice for veneer, tables and large cabinet projects.

Cedar Wood

Many people are not only familiar with cedar because of its interesting wood grain and color, but also because of its aromatic smell that repels pests and moths. The aromatic smell and insect repellent properties are why it is sometimes used in closets and lockers as a popular choice.

Cedar is also ideal for outdoor construction projects. This wood is generally considered to be resistant to decay and can withstand harsh outdoor weather well. Therefore, many people use cedar for outdoor use, such as decks, patio furniture, fences and decorative siding.

There are many different kinds of cypress in the cypress family. Certain cedar species are more suitable for specific applications than others.

Common varieties of cedar:

- Western Red Cedar
- Eastern Red Cedar
- Northern White Cedar
- Cork
- Spanish Cedar

Although many people like the aromatic properties of cedar, it is important to remember that some people may be sensitive to natural oils. If you plan to use cedar wood, it is important to wear gloves and a mask to reduce the inhalation of sawdust.

Since it is highly likely to cause irritation, Cedar should not be used as a kitchen utensil or any other item that can be used with food or in contact with the skin for a long time.

Cherry

Cherries are beautiful wood from the American black cherry fruit tree. This wood usually starts with a light pink color and will darken and become red over time. Cherry wood sometimes has dark spots, which are naturally produced by mineral deposits over time.

When choosing cherry wood, you may need to spend some time trying and make sure all the parts you choose match. Cherry can be dyed, but most people will choose its natural state, and will provide it with a clear protective layer, so that the beauty of the wood and the natural patina process produced by aging stand out.

Douglas Fir

Fir is another economical and strong cork that can be considered when starting a woodworking project. For the projects you plan to paint, fir is usually a good choice because it is sometimes difficult to dye and does not actually have a lot of wood grain.

Most fir has a very tight wood grain, which is stronger and more stable than pine. Fir is usually used in construction and public utilities projects where natural wood grain finishes are not important.

ebony

Ebony is easy to recognize because it is one of the few truly black woods. It is a very dense hardwood with many characteristics that make it required for many woodcarving and professional woodworking projects.

It is important to note that ebony is a protected species and is usually strictly regulated worldwide. Cameroon is the only country where timber can be harvested legally, and logging methods are not always ideal.

Therefore, it is sometimes difficult to obtain ebony. This tree grows very slowly, which leads to its scarcity. Historically, ebony was used in the production of musical instruments and used to make black keys in the fingerboards of pianos and guitars.

Old pianos and musical instruments that can no longer be played may be an interesting source for recycling old ebony. Antique pianos are likely to have real ebony keys, although black keys are usually made of other wood.

Ebony is used as a carving medium, which can produce a beautiful appearance and retain details. Most woodworkers recommend using only ebony hand tools, because the density and hardness may be difficult to process. For any type of work done with ebony, you will definitely want a carbide blade.

Ebony is not suitable for painting, and sometimes it may challenge the glue. In most cases, ebony is best sanded, polished, and then waxed. People should avoid using this wood as any type of sealant or varnish.

Many cabinet makers want a look similar to ebony, but when using more sustainable wood, they usually choose cherry or walnut and then dye it to dark black. Compared with ebony, this not only saves costs and promotes sustainability, but it also has far fewer challenges to build with cherry and walnut.

Hardboard (commonly known as HDF: high-density fiberboard)

Cardboard is an engineered wood product made from highly compressed wood fibers. The board can be manufactured using wet or dry processes, and the process used will determine whether the wood has two "good sides" or only one "good side."

Hard fiberboard has a clear texture and no texture pattern, so it is usually used with dyeable wood veneers. Although surface treatment is usually required to ensure that the paint will not peel or fall off in the future, cardboard can be painted.

Sometimes the blackboard is made of engineered wood such as hardwood, and then a layer of flat paint is applied. This is also a very quick and easy way to make a blackboard, and you can always use better wood as a decorative touch to build the frame.

There are many different varieties of cardboard, and different names are often used. Son stone is a kind of hard fiberboard, usually used in theater construction and props. Construction and moving companies also often use it to temporarily protect the floor surface and make it easy to move items on a trolley or trolley.

Tempered hardboard refers to the treatment of wood boards with linseed oil and then baking. This process can help make it more durable, improve moisture resistance and increase strength.

Nail board, also called perforated hard board, is a tempered hard board with holes evenly drilled into it. The diameter of these holes is usually 1/8 inch, and the spacing between each hole is usually 1/4". The pegboard is usually used for storage and as a display stand, and it is a good way to organize a garage or workbench.

Although hardboard is not the first choice for manufacturing high-end furniture, it can help increase support and strength, thereby economically manufacturing many furniture, such as the back of TV cabinets and entertainment centers. It is also often used as a backing for dressing tables and cabinets, especially because these parts are usually against the wall and are not visible.

Almost all home decoration centers provide cardboard, you can also rest assured to order online. Because engineered wood products are manufactured uniformly, you can safely order products online without worrying about defects or differences between components, just like natural wood.

Hardie board: fiber cement board

It is important not to confuse hard boards with hard boards or hard back boards. Although these names may sound confusing, they are very, very different things.

Hardie board is a composite building material and the brand name of fiber cement board. Fiber cement board is often called Hardie board because James Hardie Brand is one of the top companies that manufacture and produce this product.

Fiber cement boards are mainly made of cement and cellulose fibers. Although it is an engineered board, it is generally not classified as "wood" and cannot be used as a substitute for wood in most applications.

Fiber cement board is most commonly used as a substrate for tile floors and walls. James Hardie also produces composite fiber cement flooring and siding.

Larch/Tamarack

Larch wood, also known as tamarack wood, is a tree species of the genus Larch. Larix laricina is the most famous Tamarack variety, common in North America. In Eurasia, the species is more common larch, and more often called larch.

Technically, the larch tree is an unusual tree in the Cypress family. What makes this particular tree unique as a softwood is that it meets both softwood and hardwood standards.

It is undeniable that it is a coniferous tree with cones, but because its needles fall off in a manner similar to the way most trees lose their leaves in autumn, this tree species is also classified as a deciduous tree.

Among cork, it is one of the strongest and hardest. Since it belongs to the Cypress tree family, it has many common characteristics of Redwood and Cedar cousins.

Tamarack usually has a brownish-red hue, and is resistant to rot and pests, making it ideal for outdoor projects. The straight grain and hardness of wood make it easier to break and chip during processing.

As with Cypress family trees, it must be noted that this wood may cause irritation or allergies. The resins and oils of plants make them have excellent corrosion resistance, which may sometimes cause trouble for some people.

Therefore, these woods should generally be restricted to uses that do not come into contact with the skin for a long time. If you are using these woods, you need to make sure to take precautions to reduce the irritation of inhaling wood chips and wear gloves to limit your local contact with wood resins and oils.

Luan (also called Lauan)

Luan gum is generally considered a type of plywood, which is made from Shorea trees in the Philippines and other Southeast Asian countries. Lauan trees of the Shorea family are flowering trees. Although technically hardwood, it is likely that we will encounter wood in man-made engineering forms, such as plywood.

Such plywood is usually only available in very thin form, usually 1/8 inch thick or 1/4 inch thick. Although some stores may offer smaller pre-cuts, they are usually available in large 4'x 8'movies.

This wood is very soft and easy to bend. This gives it unique attributes and makes it very useful in building thumbnails and models. Lightweight, relatively inexpensive, and reliable availability also make it popular in other handicrafts and hobby projects.

Sometimes there are many ways to use Luan Shu, because hardwood boards are used to add stability or false effects to larger furniture, although this is usually only for "appearance" rather than actual function.

It is important to note that because the lulu tree has the willingness to bend and has a very thin shape, it should not be used in applications that bear great pressure or require structural strength.

Luan tree is sometimes called "Philippine mahogany", but it is important to know that it has a practical relationship with real mahogany, which we will introduce later.

mahogany

Mahogany is a beautiful exotic hardwood, a high-quality wood used in furniture manufacturing. Wood usually starts with a pink hue, and it gets darker and darker over time.

It is easy to use and dyes well-usually, this wood only requires a simple oil coating. Of all hardwoods, mahogany is softer than many of them, which makes your tools easier to use.

Many instrument manufacturers also use mahogany in the manufacture of guitars and pianos, because mahogany produces a clear tone.

Mahogany is usually imported from South and Central America, so it can be expensive to buy and difficult to find. These varieties are called tropical mahogany.

If you do choose to use mahogany for a project, you may want to ensure that the wood you choose continues to grow. Regrettably, if this wood is not obtained from sustainable sources, the demand for wood could lead to large-scale deforestation.

There are other types of mahogany. Australian mahogany is a plant you may encounter, it has similar characteristics, but is very different from the eucalyptus plant family. Philippine mahogany is also very different and is generally considered to be a very cheap wood like Luan.

maple

Maple is a beautiful hardwood that is often used in applications where natural wood grain is visible. Maple trees mainly grow in the sustainable forests of North America.

There are many different types of maple trees, so when buying a maple tree, you may notice that there are two basic varieties to choose from: soft or hard. Hard maple comes from sugar maple and soft maple usually comes from red maple.

Red maple, also known as soft maple, is usually the first choice for woodworking because it is much easier on tools.

Sugar maple, also called hard maple, is difficult to cut and use. Because of its hardness, sugar maple has become a very popular choice for hardwood floors. Various maple trees can be abused, resulting in no dents or wear when walking and holding furniture.

MDF: Medium Density Fiberboard

Medium density fiberboard (commonly known as MDF) is another engineered wood product, similar to HDF or high-density fiberboard, but with a lower overall density.

The difference in fiber density makes MDF more suitable for different purposes than cardboard. For example, MDF has better acoustic and insulation properties, so it is sometimes used in applications that require it, such as the interior of speakers.

Generally, MDF is not an ideal product for woodworking. This may be difficult to use, and many people worry that man-made wood products may seep into the environment with chemicals, especially formaldehyde.

If you encounter MDF, you should be aware of one of them, but In most cases, if you can avoid using MDF, you may not want to use it.

oak

Oak is perhaps one of the most popular hardwoods. It is a very popular choice for carpentry, especially in architectural furniture and high-quality heirloom works that can be passed down from generation to generation.

The two main varieties of oak wood are white oak and red oak. Red oak has a slightly reddish color and is usually the easiest to buy in most timber stores. Red oak is slightly softer than white oak, so it is easier to use when constructing.

White oak is a very hard hardwood and is an excellent choice for hardwood floors. Oak is also resistant to rot and rot, so it can be used for outdoor applications after proper treatment and sealing.

One important thing about using oak is that before using oak, it must be fully adapted to your store. Depending on the temperature and humidity conditions, oak is easy to expand and contract, so it is important to take this into consideration, especially when it is used on floors or when making containers such as wooden barrels for water.

Oak is easy to dye, so it is an excellent choice for many different dyed finishes. You can also paint oak, although most woodworkers agree that this is a waste, especially when you plan to use similar solid wood, and if you plan to paint and cover the beautiful natural wood grain, the price of this wood will be lower.

Oriented Stranded Board (OSB)

Oriented strand board, commonly known as OSB, is an engineered wood product that is often used as a substitute for plywood. Wood is made of wooden strips, which are arranged in a cross-hatched manner to bond with resin and undergo a heating process.

Wood boards are usually uniform in size and thickness, but have a very distinct texture. OSB can usually be painted, but it is difficult to avoid the wood thread texture.

You will usually find that OSB is much cheaper than plywood. Therefore, OSB usually appears in newly built houses. Many people use it as a sheath for floors, walls and roofs.

OSB is also used to construct cheap laminate furniture. In most cases, OSB has a single board attached. It is only possible to know that it is OSB where the end particles are visible.

Although these furniture are cheap, their quality is definitely lower than natural wood. A tap with a hammer may completely collapse the poorly designed OSB laminate furniture.

Therefore, most woodworkers will never use it for construction furniture, but choose to use solid wood. Although OSB is by no means the first choice for advanced carpenters, OSB can undoubtedly serve many practical purposes and is cost-effective.

OSB should not be used for external purposes. These panels usually begin to decompose after prolonged exposure to outdoor elements.

pine

Pine is a very common and versatile cork, with many practical applications. Pine trees are generally considered economical, sustainable and durable, which makes them a popular choice for many different projects.

Most pine trees grow tall and fast. They usually grow under sustainable forestry conditions, which means that the number of trees planted each year exceeds the number of trees cut down.

There are several kinds of pine trees, and they all have different characteristics. As the name suggests, southern yellow pine may have a more yellow hue than white or sugar pine varieties. White pine and sugar pine are sometimes called transparent pine.

For pine, you can decide whether to dye it, paint it or just finish it with a transparent protective sealant coating. As long as you prepare the wood correctly in advance, pine wood can be dyed well in various colors and shades.

Pine wood is sometimes found in size wood sold under the general terms "SPF wood" and "white wood". SPF stands for "Spruce, Pine and Fir".

Most pine wood is best for indoor use only, unless it is specially treated for outdoor applications, such as pressure-treated wood, which is also included in this list.

Plywood

Plywood is an engineered wood product, although it is made of solid wood. Plywood is made by gluing multiple layers of veneers together and compressing them.

Plywood can be used in many different wood finishes, and most plywood has a "good side" and a "rough side".

Plywood is available in many thicknesses, quarter-inch, half-inch, and three-quarter-inch are the sizes you are most likely to encounter in a home improvement store. Most plywood used in construction is made of fir, pine or spruce.

Pressure treated wood

The pressure-treated wood is usually yellow southern pine, which is made into wood resistant to rot and insect pests through a chemical process. Some pressure-treated wood is also made of SPF wood, which is a general abbreviation for spruce, pine and fir.

You will often see pressure-treated timber used to build decks, terraces, porch railings and other outdoor structures. Because pressure-treated wood is corrosion-resistant, it is usually possible to reuse old pressure-treated wood for new construction projects.

If you decide to use pressure-treated wood in your project, make sure to use new wood or wood produced after 2005.

Pressure treated wood used to be highly toxic and even contained toxic heavy metals such as arsenic. Fortunately, today's wood is much safer, although it is generally recommended to only use it for items that will not come into contact with food. There is a lot of controversy as to whether pressure-treated wood can be safely used on raised garden beds for growing food.

poplar

Poplar is a popular and economical hardwood that can be used in many different construction projects and applications. The wood is very light in color and may even look white. It does not have very obvious or not necessarily attractive wood grain, so poplar is often painted or used where it is not visible.

Among all hardwoods, poplar is a very soft wood, which makes it easy to process, but it also means that it can easily indent or knot during processing.

Poplars are not easy to warp or move. Since it is not the most beautiful wood, it is often used for invisible furniture parts such as drawer slides or the interior of a dresser frame.

Poplar is also often used in model making and many wooden crafts. It is easily available in most stores that sell wood, and can also be purchased in small quantities at hobby and craft stores that sell wood for wood processing projects.

Mahogany

Rosewood is music in the ears of woodworking-this wood is most commonly used to make guitars, pianos and other wooden musical instruments.

Rosewood is a peculiar hardwood, which usually makes popular musical instruments expensive. Brazilian rosewood is very common, although it can also come from Madagascar or Asia. Many people worry that illegal logging and deforestation may occur when redwood is harvested, so many people may choose other woods in their projects.

Red sandalwood is also a known irritant to many people, especially sawdust that may be produced when exposed to sawdust for a long time. If you use rosewood, it is important to use appropriate wood safety precautions.

SPF wood

SPF wood is not a specific type of wood, but a general term that includes spruce, pine and fir, which is the way the acronym of SPF is used and known.

All of these woods are cork with similar properties and characteristics, although the trained eyes are significantly different.

SPF wood is most commonly used for internal building framing and practical purposes. Because wood is a commodity, it will usually be twice the type of wood you actually get, because SPF largely depends on the current supply and demand situation.

SPF is most suitable for utility purposes or for building interior walls. Unless it is chemically modified and pressure treated, wood generally cannot withstand the harsh conditions of external use.

In most cases, SPF is usually used when the wood is invisible or exposed, such as in the case of frames. This wood can usually be sanded and smoothed for lacquering, but because stains are common, it is usually not an ideal staining method.

SPF wood is usually very cheap, but in the long run, it can sometimes cost more when trying to use it for more elaborate woodworking projects, especially if you need to spend a lot of time making the wood available for the construction you want.

When buying SPF wood, it is also important to try to buy wood from the same stack at one time, as this will increase the likelihood that at least all wood purchased will belong to the same species and have the same characteristics.

When using SPF wood in woodworking, you may want to buy more products than you think, simply because this wood is sometimes unpredictable.

It is also important to ensure that the wood has time to adapt to the humidity and temperature in the workshop to avoid large shrinkage and expansion when cutting and assembling items.

Spruce

Spruce is an evergreen softwood tree. As mentioned earlier, it is usually found in the form of "SPF timber" in logging yards and is often used in construction framing projects.

The color of spruce is very light, so it can sometimes be sold under the collective term "white wood", especially in large home decoration retail chains. It has a straight and subtle texture.

When spruce is allowed to grow to its maximum maturity, it can have excellent acoustic properties, which makes it ideal for the construction of musical instruments such as pianos, guitars and other stringed instruments.

Historically, spruce was used to make airplanes and ships. The first airplane made by Wright Brothers was made of spruce. But spruce swells easily and is not particularly weather resistant, so it is no longer commonly used in these applications.

Teak

Teak is a special hardwood of the Asian rainforest. This requires a long growth cycle, and the average tree takes 60 years to mature.

Although there are more sustainable forestry practices today than a few decades ago, this long development process means that teak will always be a hard-to-find wood, and the price is high.

Teak was originally used most often in shipbuilding, and it is still the favorite of marine craftsmen and craftsmen. It is also very popular in high-end outdoor furniture, flooring and other outdoor applications.

Teak has a natural oily appearance, which in some cases may make it difficult to stain or glue. The wood is also very hard, so you may notice that you need to sharpen and change the blade more frequently when using it.

The aroma of teak wood is described by many as very unique and simple. Many people may be very sensitive to the natural oils in teak, so it is important not to use teak for any type of application that will be in direct contact with food or skin for a long time.

When using teak, it is best to use dust masks and gloves. This will help reduce the irritation you may encounter when using wood. If you are concerned about sensitivities or allergies, it is best to avoid teak and choose a hypoallergenic wood for your project.

walnut

Walnut is a hardwood, known for its rich brown and dark colors. Walnut can be expensive and can usually only be purchased through professional wood stores, but for special projects, it is a beautiful wood.

Walnuts are relatively easy to process, but they are also very strong. It can be used for hardwood floors, although many people may still choose maple or white oak and dye these woods to match the desired walnut color because they are slightly more durable.

Walnut wood is a kind of fine wood grain, which can be polished well, and it is easy to be soiled and protected. Many people like to use it for carving, wiring and as a decorative decoration for wooden furniture. Walnut cabinets are very popular, although cheaper woods are usually dyed to match the color of walnut.

Many people are also surprised that walnuts are used in the manufacture of high-end luxury cars and guns. The fibers of walnut trees are very dense, so they can withstand impact and force the wood to withstand these types of uses.

Musical instruments such as guitars and violin are usually made of walnut. Although walnut is one of the more expensive hardwoods, it is still a more economical choice than other exotic hardwoods that produce clear tones for musical instruments.

Whitewood

"White wood" is not a specific type or type of wood, but a general term used to describe various woods with similar characteristics in strength and color.

Whitewood is the term most commonly used by large retail stores, and based on availability, they use this term in order to use one SKU number on multiple different woods. This wood can sometimes be pine, poplar or Douglas fir.

Basically, if something is sold as "white wood", you usually don't know what type of wood you will actually get. This type of wood is usually sold as dimension wood and used in construction and framing projects.

If you know the secret of identifying different types of wood, you can sometimes find some discount information about woods such as poplar and pine in the general "white wood" section, but you must also be careful because sometimes fir is also sold at a lower grade.

Whitewood is basically a "box of chocolates" in the wood world- you never know what you will get.

Zebra wood

Last but not least is the exotic wood, called zebra wood. There are several varieties of Zebrawood, most of which are native to Central America and Central Africa.

This wood is characterized by a prominent striped pattern on the wood grain. Because of its unique pattern, it is most often used in high-end furniture. This is a very heavy, hard wood, sometimes difficult to use.

Zebra wood is most often found in high-end luxury goods in history. The density and hardness make it very suitable for manufacturing such as cars, guns and other items that need to withstand shock and vibration.

Today, it is most often seen as a wood veneer used to provide decorative accents for different furniture. People are very concerned about the sustainability and legal logging of this exotic wood, so if you want to ensure that your project is environmentally friendly, you may wish to consider other hardwood alternatives.

No matter what you want to build, there is the ideal wood for you

Now that we have gone through all the different wood types and varieties for you to choose, and explained their many common uses and characteristics, we hope you can more easily choose the right wood for your project.

Whether you are building indoors or outdoors, making simple shelves or hand-carved fine art, there is the perfect wood for your project!

Tools

Carpentry means different things to different people. Many woodworkers create useful and long-lasting works to relieve stress and exercise their creativity. They are amateurs and they know that sawdust is good for the soul. Others become professionals. Their skills in building coveted furniture have been substantially compensated. However, whether you are a skilled craftsman or an amateur, you need the tools necessary for woodworking. Read the complete guide to get information about these tools. In short, the necessary tools for woodworking include:

- Chainsaw
- Handsaw
- Planes
- Sanders
- Files
- Hammer
- Mallet
- Drill
- Screw gun
- Tape measure

- Square
- Sawmill
- Workbench

Many novice woodworkers feel overwhelmed by the large number of tools available on the market. You can easily store expensive woodworking tools worth thousands of dollars in the store. However, for beginner woodworkers, most tools do not need to be sophisticated and expensive. Woodworking tools for beginners should start from the basics, so that you can feel the sense of simplicity, which is the core of a good job.

There are five basic types of woodworking tools. These are tools for cutting, finishing, assembling, measuring and fixing wooden parts, while converting raw materials into completed projects. These toolkits cover everything a woodworking beginner needs to build simple to complex projects. To help prioritize what should be placed in the basic toolbox, this is a beginner's guide to essential tools for woodworking.

Saw for woodworking

Almost every component in a woodworking project starts with cutting materials. The best and most interesting works start with rough wood. Whether it is a hardwood like oak or a softwood like pine, the wood material needs to be torn and cross-cut to form. Saws are the answer, but they are different in shape and size. They are also used for different cutting tasks. This is the condition required to start the construction of the sawmill series.

Circular saw

If every beginner's box has an electric saw, it is a circular saw. There are countless brands available, but they all have common characteristics. It is a round or round blade full of sharp teeth, which penetrate wood. All circular saws are electric, although they have various power ratings. Most are corded tools that run on household electricity, but cordless circular saws have made great progress.

Some people think that circular saws are more suitable for rough woodworking than rough woodworking. That's not true at all. In the right hand, the circular saw cuts straight, clean lines. Much depends on the blade you use.

There are three types of circular saw blades:

- Ripping blade: cut the material along the grain or longitudinally with the grain
- Cross-cutting blade: for sawing the whole grain
- Combined blade: designed for tearing and cross-cutting

The difference between the blades is their tooth design. The teeth of the serrated blade are evenly spaced, and the teeth of the transverse cutting teeth are staggered. The combined blade has two tooth types. If you need a budget, it is best to buy a high-quality combined blade with carbide teeth. You also need to know the blade diameter. The starting height of the round blade is 7½", although the common blade is 10", the diameter of 12" diameter can be used for large woodcuts.

There are two different designs of circular saws. One is direct drive, where the blade is mounted on the motor at a 90 degree angle and directly mounted on the spindle. Direct drive is the most common circular saw and also the cheapest. Worn circular saws are made for heavy work. They still have the same blade design, but the blades are driven by gears before the electric motor.

Jigsaw

Every beginning carpenter should invest in a decent Jigsaw. Because of their reciprocating motion, similar to saber saw blades, they are also called saber saws. These power tools are designed to make complex cuts, which can be straight, curved or serpentine. Think about the lines in the jigsaw, and you will know the function of the jigsaw.

The jig saw is completely different from the circular saw. Instead of rotating the blade, the jigsaw moves back and forth or up and down to cut. The number of teeth and the composition of the blade vary. They are used to cut metal, plastic and wood. Fine-toothed blades are used for sawing veneer, while coarse-toothed blades are used for roughing and fast processing.

The jigsaw is easy to operate with one hand. This way you can hold your work firmly with your other hand. The jigsaw cuts through the small and complex pieces nicely. One of the best applications for jigsaws is internal cutouts, such as internal circles or rectangles. You only need to drill a pilot hole and insert the blade. You only need to drill a pilot hole and insert the blade. With some practice, you will soon learn to cut with a jig saw.

Compound miter saw

The compound miter saw is better than the conventional circular saw. They still use the same tearing, cross-cutting and combined saw blades as circular saws. However, they are fixed to an arm or a track, just like the radial arm saws they almost have to replace. Common saw blades are 10 inches and 12 inches in diameter, but compound miter saws can be installed with smaller 7½ inches. For miter saws, always use high-quality cross-cut saw blades.

These chainsaws are extremely flexible tools. In most stores, they have replaced the standard miter box and back saw. Beginners find that the electric miter saw can cut the miter, bevel angle and compound angle much more accurately. They can be easily set to standard angles of 22½, 45 and 90 degrees, but they can be adjusted for every angle in between. This includes cutting left and right.

Electric miter saws are developed from standard cutting saws or short cut saws. They are now available in models with sliding arms that extend the cutting length. Their power heads are also tilted to both sides, which can combine bevel and bevel. Almost any angle can be cut with a compound miter saw.

Table saw

Most early carpenters invested in a table early in the game. The cutting effect produced by the table saw is difficult to achieve with other types of saws. Their design is similar to an inverted circular saw, where the saw blade is exposed from below the saw table or work surface. The depth and angle of the blade can be easily adjusted to achieve accuracy.

There are three main versions of table saws. All three are suitable for beginners. It depends on the amount of work and location you have to do. You may want to leave the stationary table saw in a store location, or store the portable saw. These are your table saw options:

- The cabinet table saw is heavy and can be placed. The origin of the name is that their electric motors are enclosed in the lower cabinet, and the blades are driven by a belt and pulley system. They are perfect for all-round work from wood renovation to panel cutting. Many beginners choose cabinet table saws as the core of their workshop.
- The desktop table saw is light in weight. They are portable, so they are ideal for moving between different locations and convenient storage when not in use. Most bench saws are directly driven. This keeps them compact, but they tend to be noisy.
- The contractor table saw is the most stringent design. Building contractors prefer them so that they can be cut quickly and easily in locations that require time and space. The contractor's table saw is also very economical, making it a good choice for beginners to learn tasks.

Band saw

Nothing can cut coarse material or perform complex bending cuts like a band saw. These power tools are a combination of a circular saw and a saber saw, in which the teeth are fixed on a continuous loop of flat steel belt and rotate around the upper and lower pulleys. A platform is installed between the pulleys, and the platform is inclined for oblique cutting.

Band saws come in many sizes. This depends on the amount of inventory to be cut and the complexity of the cut. There are two main band saw characteristics that need attention, each of which determines the size of the band saw:

- The depth capacity is the exposed distance of the band saw blade between the pulleys. It is also called face spread, and the size of a small band saw is 4 inches, and the size of a large machine is 12 inches or larger. This determines how thick your material capacity is.
- The throat depth is the distance from the blade teeth to the back of the support frame. This determines your inventory quantity. The deep throat function makes it easier to make bend cuts where it needs to be turned on the workbench.
- The serrated design allows for fast cutting, while the fine teeth allows for smooth, slower cutting. The width of the blade is important for band saws. The wide blade is more stable against tearing, while the thin blade makes bending cutting easier.

Handsaw

There will always be a hand saw in every woodworking shop. The hand saw is very easy to use and can be used for fast work or where fine cutting is required. The advantage of a hand saw is that there will be no bulky things, clumsy wires or dead batteries. The handsaw can be used at any time and is inexpensive.

Hand saws have existed for hundreds of years. They are basically toothed steel blades with wooden handles designed to slide back and forth for cutting work. But the handsaw app is much more than most beginners think. Here are some hand saw designs to consider:

- Ripping handsaw: cut into wood grain
- Cross-cutting hand saw: cut wood grain
- Combination hand saw: It can be used for both rip and cross section
- Back saw: Rectangle saw blade with serrated back plate for miter cutting
- Carcase hand saw: larger, stronger back saw
- Coping hand saws: jig saws and band saws like jig saws
- Dovetail saw: for fine dovetail joints
- keytonhole hand saw: for cutting internal holes

Woodworkers who are just starting out should invest in the highest quality hand saws they can afford. Most of the frustration of hand saws comes from cheap or dull blades. The sharp serrations have excellent teeth cutting ability and can cut wood almost as quickly and accurately as an electric saw.

Material preparation, paving and sanding materials used in wood processing

After cutting the wood chips into rough shapes, they need to do more work to give them a beautiful appearance. No matter how fine and quality your saw blade is, you still need some kind of file, planer, and sandpaper. This is what novice woodworkers should consider investing in:

Planes

The plane is a cutting tool, not a grinding or polishing device. All types of airplanes use fixed blades to scrape the wood fibers, shape them and gradually smooth them. The size and depth of the blade are key variables in how much material can be removed at one time.

You will hear some unfamiliar-sounding aircraft names (if not very interesting). Both planers and jack planers can plan wood, but their applications are quite different. You will also hear terms such as carpentry, block and razor. Again, you will hear them represented by numbers. They are all types of manual airplanes that beginners need to study. These are the manual plane ranges you may need:

- Jack Plane: These tools can remove a lot of material in one go. This is a "jack-of-all-trades" tool because both curved edge and straight edge types (for smoothing or joining respectively) can be used at the same time.
- Block Planes: These planes are small and strong. Most suitable for tight work requiring tight connections.

- Connecting plane: Same as jack planes, the difference is that they are designed to smooth the edges and connect the parts together. Usually, the joint has a long frame.
- Rabbet blade: used to cut right-angle grooves along the edge of the board. These seams are called Labert and are different from the internal grooves called Dado.
- Scraper plane: used to scrape fine fibers from the wood surface to obtain a super smooth surface effect. These planes are sometimes called cabinet scrapers.
- Spokes: a hand plane designed for curved surfaces. Initially, they were used for truck wheel spokes, but for all carpenters, they found a useful way.

Orbital sander

If you are buying an electric woodworking finishing tool, it should be an orbital sander. These fast-acting machines eliminate all the pressure caused by manual sanding and are faster. Orbital sanders are different from inline tools such as belt sanders. They use sandpaper pads that rotate in a circular or orbital pattern.

The conventional orbital sander uses a round sandpaper disc, and then rotates it once. Although they can quickly remove material, they tend to leave vortex marks that are difficult to remove. Random orbital sander is your best choice. They are not in circulation. Instead, they oscillate in a random manner, making the wooden surface silky smooth and traceless.

Hand file

Generally, there is no better tool to shape and smooth wood than a manual file. Manual files are cheap, and if you buy files made of high-quality steel, they have a long service life. Once dull, it is better to replace the hand file instead of sharpening it. Here are your main manual file options:

- Rasps are thick-edged tools with coarse teeth. They are usually used to remove large amounts of wood for integral molding, and then allow a finer file to take over.
- One side of the semicircular file is flat, and the other side is curved. This allows them to be processed on straight and curved surfaces.
- Both sides of the milling cutter file are flat. They usually have thick teeth on one side and thinner back. Milling cutter files also have serrated edges for use in narrow spaces.

Rotary cutters are similar to manual files, except that they are designed as electric drill bits. You put them in the drill chuck and let the rotating grinding action remove the material. Rotary files come in different styles and chips.

Manual files are also used for grinding other woodworking blades and drill bits. Metal files usually have very fine teeth and are made of high-grade steel. As with any tool, you usually get what you need to pay, so it is worth investing in high-end hand files.

ASSEMBLY TOOLS FOR WOODWORKING

Cutting and smoothing wood is only part of your overall woodworking process. Once your components are properly sized and smooth enough for finishes, they still need assembling. Successful woodwork assembly depends on two things. You need precision joints that will fit. You also need the right tools to assemble and securely fasten them.

These are the basic assembly tools for beginning woodworkers:

hammer

There is no universal woodworking hammer. Perhaps a carpenter's claw hammer can be compared to a tool of one size, but there are dozens of different types of tools. Usually requires a woodworking hammer to complete two tasks. That is smashed. How they accomplish this work depends on the following things:

- The head design includes face size and weight. Some hammers are very smooth, such as finishing hammers. Some jagged faces are used to hold nails and fasteners tightly, just like you see in a hammer.
- Claw design, including length and curve. The claws of the finishing hammer are long and obvious, while the framing tool uses a straighter edge to separate the material.
- The composition of the handle is critical to comfort. Most novice woodworkers prefer wooden or composite hammer handles. When struck, they have less vibration. The framer is

like a steel handle. The impact is greater, but steel adds weight, so the driving force is greater. The steel handle is not easy to break.

- Overall weight is important. The weight of the hammer is in ounces. The lightweight hammer is 8 to 10 ounces. The weight of the middle hammer is 16 to 20 ounces, while the weight of the heavy hammer is 24 to 32 ounces.

The purpose and composition of the hammer vary. Junior carpenters have many options, and you need to determine what they will do with a hammer before buying. These are the main types of woodworking hammers:

- The finishing hammer is omnipotent. This is your first purchase because they are very convenient.
- The frame hammer is very hard. However, for most woodworking projects, they are a bit too much.
- Nail hammer is like Brad driver. They are used for small jobs and usually have two different head sizes and no claws.

hammer

Don't confuse mallets with hammers. Both are compelling tools, but they have completely different applications. Hammers are usually steel-faced, but some are brass or plastic. The hammer head has a large wooden or leather head and a detachable handle to accommodate various sizes of heads.

The difference between a hammer and a mallet lies in its powerful impact and surface impression. A mallet is much softer than a hammer and absorbs impact instead of transmitting it. They also leave minimal impact marks, making the mallets great for knocking wooden joints together.

Carpenters who are just starting out should understand that you should never use a steel hammer on a chisel. The impact of the steel hammer can cause the chisel to puncture or puncture the wood, leaving a rough surface. However, hitting the chisels with a mallet can make them cut smoothly into the wood with a constant pressure.

Electric drill

Electric drill can be the best friend of novice woodworkers. Only a few old craftsmen still use props and drill bits or hand drills. For many reasons, electric drills are often used in workshops. They are not only used for drilling. You can also purchase various accessories to turn the electric drill into other tools.

If you want to buy your first electric drill, please seriously consider buying a wired model. Drill bits running at 110/120 volts have greater torque and longer service life than cordless drill bits. Some people may find the power cord blocked, but they will never let you down due to weak current.

If you want to use cordless drills, their rated voltage is. The early model was 7.5 volts, but it was quickly upgraded. Now, 18-volt cordless drill is a wise choice for beginners. They are not much more expensive than 14-volt electric drills and have greater strength.

Electric drills are also rated by their chuck size-3/8" chucks are common medium-sized, heavy-duty chucks are 1/2". There are drill bits in the key model or keyless chuck, making it easier to replace the drill bits.

Screw gun

Screws are the best all-round fastener for woodworking. They are firmly fixed and can be removed during disassembly, temporary connection or error. Of course, you don't want to have a standard manual screwdriver, but investing in a power screw gun can make screwing faster and easier. The screw gun is especially valuable when you are working with multiple screws.

The screw gun is an extension of the electric drill series. Most screw guns nowadays are cordless, which makes them very convenient. The main difference between a real screw gun and an electric drill is the internal shape of the chuck. The screw gun is designed to insert hexagonal or hexagonal drill bit shanks. This makes slippage non-existent.

Measurement and angle tools

They said to measure twice and cut once. The advice of the old carpenter is the best. Some other suggestions are to buy accurate, easy-to-read high-quality measurement equipment. The following are the main measurement and angle inspection tools needed to start carpentry:

Squares

Without the various squares, it is almost impossible to create a decent woodworking project. A good square allows you to create and verify various angles. Most squares are engraved with measurement marks on the surface. This allows them to double as measurement rules. These are the squares you should have:

- Frame square: large right-angle tool for larger work surfaces
- Try Squares: a small, right-angled handheld device that can quickly verify verticality
- Combined square: used to accurately check the angle and distance
- Speed Square: Quickly let you check 90 degree angle and 45 degree angle
- Miter-cut square: best for setting Miter-cut
- Beveled square: allows you to recreate existing angles and transfer patterns

Dividers, compasses, and depth gauges are not technically square, but they are simple and valuable woodworking tools. They entered another type of tape measure and rules.

tape measure

Every carpenter should have at least one tape measure hung on the belt.

However, it is difficult to attach all tape measures because there are many types. Here are the basic tape measures to consider:

- Telescopic steel belts: These are the most common measuring tools. Their length ranges from 12 to 30 feet.
- Flexible tape: You can use fabric or steel that is more than 100 feet in length.
- Folding rulers: Please note that they are not rulers. These are rigid measuring rods that can achieve high accuracy. Most rules are divided into multiple parts.
- Yardstick and ruler: They are in the ruler series, which is very convenient for quick take-off and straight-line placement.

Other necessary conditions for a successful woodworking project

Now that you have learned about the introductory tools needed for cutting, finishing, assembling and measuring woodworking projects, you need a way to secure them as you proceed. The clamping device is indispensable in the woodworking workshop. The sawhorse and your high-quality workbench are the two best clamping tools:

Sawmill

The sawmill is one of the first investments you should make as a woodworker. They are simple four-legged animals that can balance and support long wood lengths and heavy weights well. Saw logs are usually used in pairs, but there are six saw logs around many carpenters.

You can make your own rigid sawn timber from wood. This is an economical way to run out of waste. However, there are many commercial sawmills made of steel, fiberglass and plastic. Unless you are willing to practice, it may not be worth the time to make sawmills.

Quality workbench

If there is a real expense to consider as a carpenter, it is to invest in a high-quality workbench.

Yes, you can use 2x4 and plywood to make your own products, but you will never get the practicality brought by a professional, high-quality workbench. You will use it anytime, anywhere. The following are the functions you need to look for in the quality workbench:

- Sturdy hardwood structure
- Adjustable base for precise levelling
- Two sizes of vice
- Large working surface with built-in stop
- Lower drawer for storing tools
- Independent 360-degree channel

End

Now you have everything you need to create all the great thing you can imagine. Armed with wood, a hammer, a saw and a lot of imagination.

Create everything you want thanks to this guide.

ALWAYS REMEMBER THE SAFETY

www.ingramcontent.com/pod-product-compliance
Ingram Content Group UK Ltd.
Pitfield, Milton Keynes, MK11 3LW, UK
UKHW012248290726
14090UKWH00013B/534

9 783982 269443